THE SEVENTH SENSE

Traditionally there are five senses. The phrase, "a sixth sense", is often used to imply some super-sensitivity in a person's awareness. However, the psychologists have appropriated the "sixth sense" for the more mundane kinaesthetic sense, the awareness of one's bodily movements. My seventh sense is metacognition, the awareness of one's mental processes, the capacity to reflect on how one learns, how to strengthen memory, how to tackle problems systematically—reflection, awareness, understanding, and perhaps ultimately control. The seventh sense is a relatively undeveloped sense among people generally, and yet it may prove to be crucial to improving our capacity for learning, especially the more complex forms of learning. Some day it might even provide a key to unlock the problem of "ability", and "ability" would then be discarded as an anachronistic concept, too crude, too general, typical of the primitive psychological thinking of the 20th century.

But a claim like that is going much too far at present. All that can be claimed for metacognition is that it is likely to prove useful in the task of "learning to learn", an educational objective of increasing importance in a period of rapid technological change.

Cognitive psychology and the study skills movement

"Learning to learn" is a topic which has attracted attention from various groups adopting different lines of approach. The cognitive psychologists have followed one path, attempting by experiment to analyse the processes involved in acquiring the skills of learning. The study skills movement in schools and colleges, represented by those who offer courses on study methods and write manuals on how to study, has taken quite a different path, aiming to provide good practical advice and make it sound convincing. Neither approach has had much success in changing our established practices in learning and teaching.

The past fifteen years have seen important developments in the field of cognitive psychology. Bruner in his autobiography, *In Search of Mind* (1983), dates the renaissance from a publication by Bruner, Goodnow and Austin in 1956, describing it as "a rediscovery of the concept of mind". His work in the Centre for Cognitive Studies at Harvard was certainly seminal in putting forward the idea of the mind as active and creative, "going beyond the information given", in place of the earlier fashion of regarding psychology as a science of behaviour built up from a study of stimulus and response. But new ideas in cognitive psychology have not got through to education. Much of the experimental work has been done with the mentally handicapped, and has concentrated on memory and information processing rather than learning. The tasks chosen for their laboratory studies are usually artificial exercises (such as paired associate learning), designed to be measureable rather than meaningful, in which even the subjects of the experiments may not know the purpose of the tasks they are set. The conclusions from recent experimental research have been applied to what is called "intellectual skills training", as the cognitive psychologists call it. The terminology in this area of information technology is complex and forbidding: Sternberg's (1983) "programme of intellectual skills training", for example, "provides explicit training in both executive and non-executive information processing". (To help you understand what that means, he analyses executive processes as: "problem identification, process selection, strategy selection, representation selection, allocation of resources, solution monitoring, sensitivity to feedback, translating feedback into action, and implementation". Non-executive processes are: "selective encoding, selective combination, inference, mapping, application, comparison and justification".) Not surprisingly, this kind of research has had relatively little impact on what actually happens in schools.

Developments in the schools, in contrast, in the form of teaching study skills, have been practical and down-to-earth. If psychological research is over-complex, the study skills movement is simplistic in its assumptions. It assumes that if you want people to learn how to learn, you teach them; and if you are not sure what to teach, then you follow "good practice" and do what everyone else is doing. Study skills are usually taught to university entrants or to senior pupils going on to higher education, as if study skills were not likely to be required by others. Moreover, study skills tend to be directed towards techniques of passing examinations rather than learning more effectively. Being aimed at the over-16s, the attempt to provide training in learning may be too late to change habits which have already become firmly established.

But the main criticism of the study skills movement is that it lacks a sound rationale. Manuals on study have been published since 1900, and the advice has changed little over the years. This wouldn't matter if the advice were sound. But much of it lacks any empirical basis (except perhaps the rote-learning experiments of Ebbinghaus in the 1890s): it is "self-perpetuating material based on general consensus" (Maddox, 1962), encouraging the myth of the ideal student as a model of organised efficiency. The manuals of the 1920s seem obsessed with details of study environment, procedural routines and regular habits; sixty years later we are still advised on the wattage of reading lamps, the use of different coloured pens for note-taking and how to get good grades by using plastic binders for your project reports, followed by vague horatory paragraphs on motivation and interest, with rallying calls for improvement. Few of the successful scholars we know, the original thinkers and writers, possess the good habits and virtues of the model pupil in the study manuals.

However, recent research has put study skills on to a more promising track, recognising that study methods are best developed in the natural context of school work, not as a separate collection of techniques. For example, the recent NFER project by Tabberer and Allman (1983) concludes that study skills should

"be conceived as the provision of support for the study problems that students already encounter in their subject classes, (with) content and approach...closely linked to the actual problems that students have, carefully planned to augment the teaching and learning which students already regard as important".

Our concern, as we review research in cognitive psychology and the study skills movement in schools, is that these two lines of development are proceeding independently, as if neither had anything to contribute to the other. Can we perhaps translate the important new ideas in cognitive research into terms which are relevant to school and college work? This became the aim of our "Learning Strategies" project.

Learning to Learn

The idea of "learning to learn" has come to have considerable importance as an aim of education. For the advocates of continuing education, it is the prime task of the school. In a modern world where a person in a skilled job will change that skilled job drastically three times on average in a working life, schools and colleges cannot just equip young people with skills to keep them going for the rest of their career: formal education must foster the most important skill of all, the skill of learning. Whatever words are used to express the idea, learning to learn is seen as an underlying aim from pre-school to university. The Robbins Report (1963), in the section on "The aims of higher education", stated:

"What is taught should be taught in such a way as to promote the general powers of the mind."

The Hale Report (1964) on "University Teaching Methods", stated:

"The aim and nature of the undergraduate course should be not only or even primarily to equip the student with knowledge, but also, and more importantly, to teach him to think for himself and to work on his own."

The Aberdeen University pamphlet on "Techniques of Study" which I wrote in 1962 (and which is still in circulation) expresses the point at its simplest:

"Developing an efficient technique of work and study during your student years provides you with a skill which will be valuable throughout your professional life."

Of course it is not only the university student for whom learning to learn is important. It is, or should be, an underlying aim at all stages of education. But how does one set about learning to learn? Can it be taught? Even if it is in the category of "things which may be learned but cannot be taught", we cannot afford just to leave it to chance; we need to consider how best to encourage students and children to learn how to learn. What does that involve?

Part of the answer is that learning to learn involves bringing the process of learning to conscious level and thus gaining control over the organisation (or orchestration) of our learning. We have to get beyond cognition, into what is termed "metacognition", in order to look at what cognition is. Metacognition is my seventh sense.

At this stage, I have to introduce some of the jargon, to provide a structure for reviewing what is involved in learning to learn. Sternberg's "executive processes", which I mentioned earlier, represent one group of components in learning. Cognitive psychologists such as Flavell, Belmont and Butterfield use the phrase "the *executive functions* of cognition" to describe the organising processes of the mind. In learning, the executive

4

functions are the decision-making processes which determine how we set about the task of learning. People make these decisions for themselves unthinkingly, often unaware that they have a choice, unaware of what they are doing or why. For most people—even some university students—the method of learning is "no method": you expose yourself to the possibility of learning—by reading or listening or watching or sometimes just attending classes—and you hope that learning will take place. Of course it does, but often very inefficiently. When we asked children in primary school how they learned, they said they learned "by going to school", "by doing their lessons", "by being taught". The more sophisticated students and older children may be able to identify certain techniques of learning, but usually only some specific procedures which they were once taught or which once proved successful, and they persevere with the procedures even where they are inappropriate; or they copy the style of someone they use as a model, such as a parent, a teacher, an older sibling or a friend.

Perhaps a computing analogy will help to explain "executive functions". The effectiveness of a computer depends not only on its machine capacity (the hardware), but also on the quality of the programs (the software); and good programs may sometimes be used inefficiently by an operator. If "hardware" is equivalent to our intelligence or ability, and "software" is the programs we have learned to apply, then the "executive functions" are the programming. When there is a failure in learning, we tend to blame the hardware; but failure may be due to the lack of a program, or to selection of the wrong program by the operator.

Expressing this in technical terms, when children perform badly, we usually attribute this to a *mediational deficiency*, that is, lack of skill or knowledge or intellectual capacity. But poor performance may also be due to a *production deficiency*: children may have a necessary skill but yet be unable to use that skill appropriately, that is, be unable to select or retrieve the appropriate skill when it is needed. Training in "executive functions" can be seen as a means of remedying such production deficiencies: it may not eliminate differences in capacity for learning or ability, but it can make a contribution towards reducing the over-riding effect of individual differences.

The computer analogy may be misleading, for in human learning we cannot separate the machine capacity, the program and the processing by the operator. We program ourselves, and, as Belmont and Butterfield (1977) observe, the executive functions of

5

cognition are "the means by which people manage simultaneously to be programmers and processors". Gaining control of the executive functions is the key to success. But

> "No one yet knows how to train executive functions....The executive is currently almost a total mystery, and we are sure it will be the object of a great deal of research in cognitive development."

Metacognition

Perhaps we can unravel some of the mystery if we look to that seventh sense. John H Flavell at Stanford University is credited with the introduction of the term, "metacognition", in 1970, to describe the monitoring of one's thinking which is (or could be, if it is developed) our seventh sense.

> "Metacognition refers to one's knowledge concerning one's own mental processes....For example, I am engaging in meta-cognition if I notice that I am having more trouble learning A than B; if it strikes me that I should double-check C before accepting it as a fact; if it occurs to me that I had better scrutinize each and every alternative in any multiple-choice type task situation before deciding which is the best one; if I sense that I had better make a note of D because I may forget it....Meta-cognition refers...to the active monitoring and consequent regulation and orchestration of these processes usually in the service of some concrete goal or objective" (Flavell *et al*, 1970)

More recently, Flavell (1979) has distinguished four classes of phenomena: metacognitive knowledge, metacognitive experiences, metacognitive goals and metacognitive strategies (see Brown (1984) for summary). The first example in the quotation above is in the category of metacognitive experience; the others are metacognitive strategies. Metacognition is thus not just monitoring or awareness, though that is a necessary first condition: it also extends to the orchestration of processes. The analogy of a seventh sense fits because our senses are not passive receptors but interact selectively and constructively with our environment to enable us to regulate and direct our behaviour. Ann Brown (1978) at the Center for the Study of Reading in the University of Illinois, comments:

> "In the domain of deliberate learning and problem-solving situations, conscious executive control of the routines available to the system is the essence of intelligent activity."

This is the kind of promise offered by research in the area of metacognition. Conscious regulation is "the essence of intelligent activity". People will learn more effectively if they can establish "conscious executive control of the routines". If intelligence is defined as capacity for learning, perhaps one might dare to suggest that people will be more intelligent if they can develop the seventh sense. Geoffrey Brown (1984) in a recent paper speculates on the goal of basing a school curriculum on "essential metacognitive skills which improve the efficiency of the children's cognitions". But, he concludes: "That goal is still some way ahead".

Some way ahead?

If we are to translate these aspirations into practical terms of application to teaching and learning, then we must analyse the concepts and elaborate the processes much more thoroughly. It is a formidable task. When I tell you that we are trying to work out the applications to the curriculum for children in the age-range 10-14, you will understand why this research (which the Scottish Education Department has funded) has to be classified as a "high risk" project.

Some of our critics question the choice of the 10-14 age group, saying the task would be more practicable with university students. Others have argued that it would be more appropriate to the under-5s. But by age 10, most children have the basic tolls of school work, and are beginning to establish habits in their cognitive processes which may be difficult to change later. They are also entering the pre-pubertal stage in which there is an awareness of self which we might be able to turn to advantage. What happens at present in these years at school? The last two years at primary school are often taken up with routine work which is intended to establish and practise certain narrowly defined skills. In the first two years of secondary school, teachers demand a massive volume of rote-learning to master the new 'vocabulary' and concepts of specialist subjects. Thus the period 10-14 imposes a heavy pressure to conform to prescribed modes of working, thinking, and learning—with little provision for thinking for oneself or for the interpretation of skills which lie at the basis of 'learning to learn'. Thus an opportunity is lost, and it is not surprising that many pupils are 'turned off' from learning for good. If we could inject some element of 'learning to learn' into the curriculum of those years, the benefits might be wide ranging.

But how? We think there is more mileage in trying out the ideas in classrooms than in further theoretical analysis. Practical trials may point the way to the refinement of theory. But first we have to communicate the ideas to teachers, and to do this we have to be clear ourselves about our definitions of terms such as "skills" and "strategies".

Skills and strategies

Schools teach skills, in set contexts and for specific purposes. We believe that schools should teach learning strategies. Some teachers will say that they are doing this already. That depends on what we mean by "strategies" and "skills". We adopt a hierarchical model which distinguishes *skills*, *strategies* and *approach* to learning, each level being generalised from the preceding one (see Figure 1).

Level 3 SPECIFIC *SKILLS*	Skills specific to subjects, or general skills specific to tasks shared in related subjects
Level 2 LEARNING *STRATEGIES*	Superordinate skills, generalised procedures or sequences of activities with a conscious purpose
Level 1 *APPROACH* to LEARNING	Intelligent regulation of learning, self-monitoring selection of strategies, insight through reflection

Figure 1. A hierarchical model of skills, strategies and approach.

At Level 3 there is a whole range of skills and sub-skills which are involved in learning. Many of these skills are taught and learned in the context of specific subjects or specific situations: Algebra is an example, which even in a primitive form can improve primary school pupils' ability to handle numerical problems. Similarly, there are scientific concepts and methods and principles, and skills in applying these, which improve our competence. Maps in geography, diagrams and charts as modes of representation, perspective in drawing, the use of a lathe or a dictionary or an index, the use of computers, and at a basic level, skills in reading, writing and number: these are all taught and learned. These are Bruner's "amplifiers". (Attitudes, of confidence or the opposite, also are learned, but for the present let us limit the analysis to the cognitive area.)

8

Level 2 is the start of learning to learn, and it involves building these skills into more generalisable strategies and learning to use these with a conscious purpose, not just on instruction or demand. "Generalisable" implies transfer from the context in which they are learned into new contexts. Some skills obviously are more transferable (or versatile) than others: perspective in drawing for example is rather limited, while diagrams and algebraic representation have wider potential. I use the term "strategies" to indicate a level above that of skills, putting the skills together. Strategies are different from skills in that a strategy has an element of conscious purpose; a strategy is a sequence of activities rather than a unitary event; and strategies are considered to be more modifiable and flexible in nature, whereas skills are more "reflexive" (Kail and Bisanz, 1982). Duffy (1982) defines strategies as "secret algorithms of learning". In order to apply a strategy, you must possess a range of skills and be aware of a range of possible strategies and make an appropriate selection from these. This implies the capacity to transfer skills and strategies to fit new situations not previously encountered.

Level 1 represents a generalisation from the strategies at Level 2. It is the intelligent monitoring and regulation of one's learning, thinking abstractly about what is required, and what one is doing, and how these match. We originally used the term "learning style" for this, but we now find the word "approach" causes less confusion.

In formal education, Level 3 is taught thoroughly. Level 1, if it is taught at all, is usually the aim of "study skills" courses, taught by counselling staff, unrelated to Levels 2 or 3. Level 2, the pivot of the system, is left to chance. We don't know much about what Level 2 comprises, how to teach it, or how it is learned, or whether it can be taught. But our suggestion is that the skills at Level 3 should be taught in such a way as to cultivate the more general strategies of Level 2, and similarly the strategies of Level 2 are integrated to develop the approach of Level 1. Each level must be related to the others, so that learning to learn is embedded firmly in mainstream teaching, and not imparted as an extra in one or two inspiring talks or vague exhortations as part of a study skills curriculum.

Perhaps it is wrong to say that Level 2 strategies are "left to chance". Figure 2 offers a list of strategies for the efficient completion of most school tasks; the usual response from teachers is, "We do this already."

1. Orientation to the task:	asking what does the situation demand, defining hypotheses, establishing the aims and parameters of a task.
2. Planning:	sketching an outline, deciding on tactics within a set timetable, selecting and sequencing appropriate procedures.
3. Monitoring:	the continuous attempt to match efforts and products against the initial questions or purposes.
4. Checking:	scrutiny of results against preliminary estimations and approximations.
5. Revising:	redrafting, recalculation, to remove errors and confusions, to polish and improve, redefining objectives.
6. Self-testing:	final self-assessment of results and of performance on task.

Figure 2. Strategies for efficient completion of school tasks

Individually, these are familiar strategies which many teachers encourage, but they tend to be taught in specific contexts— planning for projects, checking for arithmetic, self-testing for spelling, and so on. The missing element in conventional teaching is *transfer*, the capacity to generalise, selecting skills learned in one context to apply in a new and different context.

Transfer

There are four criteria to be met in skills training:

1. Mastery: the initial acquisition of the skill;
2. Retention: the capacity to call up and reproduce the skill subsequently;
3. Durability: long-term retention;
4. Transfer: the ability to apply the skill in an appropriate new context.

Schools tend to concentrate on the first three of these, and neglect the last. The skills of simple mathematics are well taught to the level of mastery in the primary schools, and are subsequently over-learned through repetition and drill and exercises for durability; but transfer is not so adequately catered for. Transfer, in the words of Belmont and Butterfield (1977), is the *sine qua non* of "genuine structural change".

"Unless a child exhibits activity akin to the trained activity in some situation other than the training task, he has done nothing but parrot the instructor."

10

Transfer is "the real acquisition of generalised cognitive functions".

Those who remember the "transfer of training" controversy of the 1930s will recall the two main findings which were eventually established: transfer is most likely to occur (a) when stress is laid on common elements in the training situation and in the related area to which the learning is applied; and (b) when we deliberately teach for transfer. How then should we teach for transfer? This is a crucial question, and a vital part of our argument.

Children can be taught specific strategies for tackling various kinds of tasks in their school work—like rote-learning, using a reference book, planning a piece of writing, answering a comprehension exercise or checking computation. "Transfer" involves the capacity to apply the strategies implicit in these procedures more generally to situations other than those for which the procedures were learned initially. For this to happen, the strategies must first be consciously articulated and practised so that eventually they become part of one's habitual unconscious approach to learning.

The two requirements in that last sentence provide the key to the teaching of strategies: "conscious articulation" and "practice". Conscious articulation takes us back to metacognition, being aware of what we are doing in the process of learning. Practice is necessary because of the limited "channel capacity" of human memory.

There are various ways of describing our limited channel capacity. Miller (1956), for example, gave a precise figure: the number of things we can keep in mind at one time is seven, plus or minus two. Case (1978) suggested the concept of limited "M-space" in the child's brain which restricts the number of factors which can be held, balanced and analysed at any one time. Familiarisation with routines means that they require smaller M-space, so the learning of strategies frees space for attention to be given elsewhere. This is a basic rule in acquiring athletic skills or manual dexterity. The response must be practised until it becomes part of one's habitual unconscious approach to learning. Otherwise, like the centipede in the well-known story, by thinking about what you are doing you inhibit your capacity to do it. For these reasons, then, if we are correct in our analysis, learning to learn must begin at an early age, and practising learning strategies is a prime element in the curriculum of the years from 10 to 14.

Teachers know about the value of practice, but are less familiar

11

with "conscious articulation". This involves identifying the variety of sub-skills which are then built into sequences or strategies for tackling problems. Bereiter (1975) and Scardamalia (1981) in Ontario have developed teaching procedures which emphasise both the "practice" and the "conscious articulation" elements needed for transfer. Task analysis is undertaken first, as a preliminary stage in helping pupils approach tasks which appear superficially simple but actually call upon a wide range of sub-skills. Then they advocate the isolation and practice of these component skills so that through rehearsal they will demand less attention. Otherwise, they demand too much of the limited attention available, and thus inhibit an effective response.

Our own research included an investigation of how far strategies were being taught or learned, and whether teachers and learners alike were able to "articulate consciously" the processes involved. Our original plan was to interview children aged 10-14, encouraging them to introspect about the business of learning. Many children seemed blissfully unaware that there *was* any procedure at all in learning. They did what was required of them—or rather what they thought the teacher wanted: teachers teach, and as a result children learn. Even where children did demonstrate some sophistication in their metacognitive knowledge, they often showed little evidence of putting these processes into action when faced with the demands of tasks set by their teachers. A classic case of production deficiency? Or were the children just being wiser than us in realising that classroom tasks are most efficiently performed and best rewarded by using the least sophisticated strategies geared to following instructions and getting finished in good time?

We attempted to explore this further by setting out to look for examples of classrooms where children were being set or offered significant challenges which would develop their use of strategic thinking. Local authority advisers helped by suggesting schools which, they said, were already doing what we were looking for. This led to a phase of classroom observation which was time-consuming (though interesting). This too got us nowhere. Even in these "best" schools, there were few open questions (see Galton *et al*, 1980 and Wragg, 1984, for similar findings); there were many time-filling tasks and much "busy work" which did not demand mental effort. There was reinforcement and over-learning, but we did not often find the teaching or encouragement of strategies which we were looking for. Of the criteria listed above, we found emphasis on mastery and retention, and sometimes durability, but not transfer.

Developing learning strategies

Recently, we have worked with two small groups of teachers, first with a group of both primary and secondary school teachers, later with a group of primary teachers only, to see if the teachers *could* create the kind of learning situations which our analysis suggested were necessary for learning to learn. We compiled a manual of exemplars, suggested lines of development, and prepared materials; the teachers wrote frank and critical comments, and also offered descriptions of their own attempts to teach strategies (for it was part of our plan to encourage them to try it themselves). Some teachers were dubious at first, and later thought it was a great idea. Others started thinking it was a promising idea, and later thought it was too difficult for the children—and also too difficult for the teacher.

The outcome of our work with the teachers is a tentative three-part description of teaching approaches which might improve children's capacity to think and work strategically, namely:

1. Direct training of strategies;
2. Modelling of strategies;
3. Encouraging metacognitive skills.

1. Direct training

Procedures for problem-solving are traditionally part of the teacher's stock-in-trade: identify the category of problem, select the appropriate method of attack, check the result. There has been a lot of American work on this approach to learning which deserves to be better known in Britain (see, for example, O'Neil's *Learning Strategies*, 1978), varying from complex analyses to simple algorithms, of which the best known is probably Robinson's (1946) SQ3R guide for reading. The value of these procedures is that, once they become automated, they keep the learner on target without occupying scarce "M-space" in the brain. However, if they are taught as tricks to cope with specific tasks, their value is limited. If the learner is to have the capacity for transferring the strategy, for applying the procedures in new situations, the teaching must not be mechanical but must stress the potential for transfer. Combining this requirement for flexibility with the need for practice so that the procedure becomes automated, is no easy task. Direct teaching of strategies is not the easy option which it may seem at first sight.

2. Modelling

Copying the actions and style of a person who is respected or in authority, whom we wish to please or on whom we are dependent, is a basic intuitive method by which children (and adults) learn modes of behaviour. Verbalising—talking aloud as one works— can bring this intuitive process into consciousness and thus under control. Vygotsky's (1962) analysis of how children internalise their parents' verbalising provided the basis for a modelling approach suggested by Meichenbaum and Goodman (1971) for improving learning procedures:

   (i) the teacher models her own strategy on a task, describing aloud how she works;

  (ii) the child then works through the task, repeating the same or similar verbal controls and reflections;

 (iii) the child practises the procedure until the verbalisation becomes automatic and internalised.

"One can imagine a similar training sequence in the learning of a new motor skill such as driving a car. Initially the driver actively goes through a mental checklist, sometimes aloud, which includes verbal rehearsal, self-guidance, and sometimes appropriate self-reinforcement....Only with repetition does the sequence become automatic and the cognitions become short-circuited. This sequence is also seen in the way children learn to tie shoelaces...."

The American author on children's writing, Donald Graves (1983), provides an example of modelling in the teaching of writing. Graves uses "the conference-drafting approach", in which children are encouraged to confer and draft and redraft several times. The teacher models the process, sitting down and writing when the children do, composing on large sheets or overhead projector with commentary.

"The objective of composing before children is to make explicit what children ordinarily can't see: how words go down on paper, and the thoughts that go with the decisions made in the writing."

The purpose is "not to beat the child over the head with a new skill", but to show how to "select skills within the context of natural predicaments".

14

3. *Encouraging metacognitive skills*

The critical tests for any of these training methods are (i) whether learners can remember and maintain the skills or strategies on later occasions; and (ii) whether children have the capacity to transfer or generalise what has been taught to related but not totally similar situations. The first of these conditions is fairly easy to meet; the second is much harder. Improving the capacity to transfer is the particular contribution which metacognition can provide. Awareness of one's mental processes, and skill and practice in self-monitoring, are the means by which the direct instruction can be decontextualised, and the control can be passed from the instructor to the learner, so that the learner takes a more active and responsible part in the process.

Various workers in USA and Australia (see Flavell 1981, and Baird and White 1984, for example) are currently trying to devise means of encouraging metacognitive skills in the classroom. One of our own suggestions took the introduction of computers into schools as an opportunity to try out some of these ideas in a new situation, free from the dead hand of traditional methods. Working with computers, children are on their own, and must think for themselves; but they also need instruction to get started. There is scope here for direct instruction on strategies, and for modelling, but also for metacognition, which begins as an attempt to understand the processes of the operator, by asking: what do I need to do to win in this computer game? what have I done wrong? are there any procedures which can guide me to mastery of this task?

Further questions

This is an unfinished story, with many questions still to be answered. Are these suggestions practicable? Can teachers be persuaded to apply and develop them? Are they likely to be effective?

Can a core curriculum be constructed around "essential meta-cognitive skills", as Brown (1984) suggested? If so, at what stage? Age 17 or 18 is surely too late, but does one have to wait for the spontaneous generation of metacognitive skills in adolescence or can they be taught or encouraged prior to this? Will improved metacognition result from *challenges* to the child's thinking by difficult tasks and problems, or will it only occur when the child is so familiar with the type of task that processing skills are automated and leave 'spare' capacity for metacognition?

15

Flavell's (1981) answer to that last question is that we need "space" to think:

> "The more complex and cerebral forms of metacognitive experiences (eg actively trying to figure out *why* you do not understand something versus merely noticing *that* you do not understand it) place heavy demands on attention and occupy considerable space in working memory. Consequently, you are more likely to have these kinds of experiences when attention and memory resources permit (eg when you have sufficient time to think about your cognitions, when you are not in a highly emotional state, and the like)."

What this also tells us of course, is the sorts of conditions under which metacognition (and, by implication, the development of learning strategies) is likely *not* to take place. Consider the situation where little or no conscious thought is required to process instructions and perform a task; where you are not stretched by new material or problems; where you are not required to assess and monitor your own progress and performance; where the principal demands are for 'busy' work in an overcrowded examination syllabus. Unfortunately, this sounds depressingly like a description of the average school classroom!

Conclusion

Learning to learn is still elusive, though all subscribe to its importance. The seventh sense is, to use Brown's phrase, "still some way ahead".

However, I hope the topic is appropriate to this occasion, even though it is a speculative paper, exploring ideas, which might not satisy the calls for "relevance", the current fashionable criterion for research. The seventh sense is, admittedly, in a different category of research from grade-related criteria in secondary school examinations; but it may prove its relevance in time when grade-related criteria are dead and gone. Whatever you may think of the particular area which I have chosen to speak of, I hope you will agree that, in the work of SCRE and the activities of SERA, and in educational research generally, there must always be a place for exploratory work of this kind. For ourselves, we are glad to have had a small part in the development of a topic which will surely be a dominant theme in the years that lie ahead.

REFERENCES

Baird J R and White R (1984). *Improving learning through metacognition: a classroom study*, Paper to AERA Conference, New Orleans, April 1984.

Belmont J M and Butterfield E C (1977). "The instructional approach to developmental cognitive research", in Kail, R V and Hagen, J W, (eds) *Perspectives on the Development of Memory and Cognition*, Erlbaum, Hillsdale, N J.

Bereiter C and Anderson V (1975). *Thinking Games*, Ontario Institute for Studies in Education, Occasional Papers, 16.

Brown A (1978). "Knowing when, where, and how to remember: a problem of metacognition", in Glaser, R (ed) *Advances in Instructional Psychology*, Book 1, Erlbaum, Hillsdale, N J.

Brown G (1984). "Metacognition: New Insights or Old Problems?" *British Journal of Educational Studies*, in press.

Bruner J (1983). *In Search of Mind*, Harper & Row, New York.

Bruner J S, Goodnow J J, and Austin G A (1956). *A Study in Thinking*, Wiley, New York.

Case R (1978). "Piaget and beyond: towards a developmentally based theory and technology of instruction", in Glaser, R (ed) *Advances in Instructional Psychology* Book 1, Erlbaum, Hillsdale, N J.

Duffy G (1982). "Fighting off the alligators: What research in real classrooms has to say about reading instruction", *Journal of Reading Behavior*, 14, 4 357-373.

Flavell J H (1979). "Metacognition and cognitive monitoring: a new area of cognitive-developmental inquiry", *American Psychologist*, 34, 906-911.

Flavell J H (1981). "Cognitive monitoring", in Dickson, W P (ed) *Children's Oral Communication Skills*, Academic Press, New York.

Flavell J H, Friedrichs A G, and Hoyt J D (1970). "Developmental changes in memorization processes", *Cognitive Psychology*, 1, 324-340.

Galton M, Simon B, and Croll P (1980). *Inside the Primary Classroom*, Routledge & Kegan Paul, London.

Graves D (1983). *Writing: Teachers and Children at Work*, Heinemann, London.

Hale Report (1964). *University Teaching Methods*, HMSO, London.

Kail R V and Bisanz J (1982). "Cognitive strategies", in Puff, C R (ed) *Handbook of Research Methods in Humary Memory and Cognition*, Academic Press, New York.

Maddox H (1962). "An analysis of how-to-study manuals" (abstract), *Bulletin of the British Psychological Society*, 47, page A29.

Meichenbaum D and Goodman J (1971). "Training impulsive children to talk of themselves: a means of developing self-control", *Journal of Abnormal Psychology*, 77, 115-126.

Miller G A (1956). "The magical number seven, plus or minus two: some limits on our capacity for processing information", *Psychological Review*, 63, 81-97.

O'Neil H F (ed) (1978). *Learning Strategies*, Academic Press, New York.

Robbins Report (1963). *Higher Education* (Cmnd 2154), HMSO, London.

Robinson F P (1946). *Effective Study*, Harper, New York.

Scardamalia M, Bereiter C, and Fillion B (1981). *Writing for Results: a Sourcebook of Consequential Composing Activities*, Ontario Institute for Studies in Education, Curriculum Series, 44.

Sternberg R J (1983). "Criteria for intellectual skills training", *Educational Researcher*, 12, 2, 6-12 and 26, February 1983.

Tabberer R and Allman J (1983). *Introducing Study Skills: an Appraisal of Initiatives at 16 +*, NFER-Nelson, Windsor.

Vygotsky L S (1962). *Thought and Language*, Wiley, New York.

Wragg E C (ed) (1984). Classroom Teaching Skills, Croom Helm, London.